Kali's Lament
&
Other Poems

Anita Saran

BookLeaf Publishing

India | USA | UK

Presentation by *BookLeaf Publishing*

Web: www.bookleafpub.com

E-mail: info@bookleafpub.com

ISBN: 9789363314009

First edition 2024

To Daddy Who Always Knew

PREFACE

The short story City of Victory was narrated by actress Badria Timimi on BBC Radio 4 in 2001. It then grew into a novella of the same name and was first published by Chillibreeze.com. Today it is a prose poem. You can find the novella version on Amazon India.

All the paintings in this collection are the author's creation. A professional artist, Anita has held four solo shows of her paintings in Bangalore. The last one, 'Sarandipity Perspectives', was held at Chitrakala Parishad, Bangalore, in March 2024. Her art has been featured in the Museum of Art and Photography (MAP) in Bangalore.

Antara Unleashed - The Mist

Wars rage in the world, militants behead babies, people fry eggs on top of cars, animals disappear never to be seen again, birds fall dead from the sky, ancient viruses reawaken after centuries from melting glaciers, eating their way into brains and guts, and I seek refuge in my God, in those magical, tumultuous teenage years when there was no internet, no television, no responsibilities, no tsunami waiting to rear its head, no endangered sunsets.

It is 1976, and I am chugging my way to college in Darjeeling on the little blue toy train. The ride is like the slow, tantalising drip of jungle honey. So slow I can walk alongside, on the brink of the hills, green valleys yawning below, chew on delicate pink flowers with a sour taste, and breathe deep, the pine-scented air steadily growing colder.

Ah, the Darjeeling of my childhood holidays! The rhododendrons, the large creamy magnolias, the Kanchenjunga mountains aflame in the sunset, the steep streets that take your breath away, the shops overflowing with primitive amber and silver dragons with turquoise eyes.

The college is a fairytale castle with soaring towers. On the green lawns, so steep you can roll down them, wild roses grow unprompted, pink and small in round, calculated flower beds.

In the cemetery with its marble tombstones at the bottom of the hostel gardens, there is no fear, no grief, but bell-like purple flowers, the cool pine-scented breeze, and a gentle light filtering through tall trees. I like to read and dream here beneath the feathery pines.

The path leading down to the cemetery is slippery with moss, and I tread carefully. Below this final resting place, the earth drops into a wholesome scene: small houses exhaling smoke from chimneys, fat red cows with tinkling bells and bangs on their foreheads, and rosy-cheeked children with runny noses playing their childish games.

The hostel is an old British building filled with air and light and gleaming with polished wooden floors on which we dance barefoot in the evenings, not so much with each other as with ourselves. The great windows invite escape. After all, college means freedom.

The haunting, fiery beauty of Yeats' Leda and the Swan' bursts upon me from the lips of the

Irish Mother Damien, making the hair rise on my arms. She is sharp and kind.

Seeing how charmed I am by a room at the end of a corridor, she lets me have it. The windows overlook a school courtyard and far beyond, green, beckoning hills that must hold faerie.

The washman lives on the edge of our little hill in a hut that looks like it is about to fling itself into the valley below. I love the precipitous walk to this ramshackle home. It is warm inside, the air sweet with the breath of a cow and her calf. I kiss the mottled white and brown calf on its velvety face. I like large, black wet noses and the huffing and puffing of sweet, sugary breath down my neck.

My best friend, Tika, is strange. She claims to have dropped to Earth from another planet. She does have a lump—a hump really—on her back, which bulges through her clothes. Her parents, she alleges, found her as a baby in their garden and did not love her. Her eyes are deep pools of sorrow even when she laughs. Tika and I go riding together. Two lost souls fused together with the poetry of rejection and rebellion. We gallop down those roads from some dream, and our lives fall from our lips in a torrent.

"Look," she yells past the wind, "there's the guy who's been following you around like some faithful hound!" He is watching us gallop by. Gold-brown eyes, tight-curled hair, Adonis nose, full lips, French beard. Sinewy arms showing from rolled-up denim sleeves. Heavy coil of rope slung across a broad shoulder. And I am glad my wavy hair is long enough for the wind to play with, whipping streaks of my red lipstick across my cheeks in a blush.

There is no fear here. No love greater or more elusive than one born in the roiling mists of Darjeeling, to seep into the souls of those holding hands in secret lover's lanes.

Antara Unleashed - Mirage

'The Man Who Cried' paints a sad world—a
little girl, forced to bid farewell to a father
leaving for America. Tears trace familiar paths
on my cheeks. Tomorrow, the ocean of time
throws up another shard—the anniversary of
your death.

On the train to our ancestral home, where we
had hoped to nurse you at least for a few months
more, you were only an item number in the
luggage van, and the rhythmic clatter of the train
failed to lull me to sleep. Words spilled out of
me:

The yellow leaves of autumn fall
And you, my father
Still young, still green
An untimely wind has swept you away
The smile upon your shrunken face
Death-defying

How can I sleep when you, my father
Lonely god, I never knew
Despite our love
Yonder lie
Anointed with chloroform?
My fingers benumbed with pain
Will lay the flowers of life
On your sad shell

To wither
In the consuming flame
As woman I am not meant to see
And that is as it should be
For how could I bear to look
Upon the fire's greed
The sacred waters
That cannot wash you away?

You killed him! They shriek
With your youth in rebellion
Abandoned by a cruel Medea
When you were a child!
Your sorrow killed him
Yet left you cold.
Again and again, he died for you
While you laughed
Your laugh of innocence...

Yet in another realm
Night never comes
Over lakes of still water
White lotus opens
And all is radiance!
A song brings you to life
The scent of your cologne
Your letters crisp with memories...
Hush! Keep your mind still
Still as the trees

Untouched by the breeze
The silent, sprouting earth.

And so, as the little girl on screen seeks her
father across the ocean, I too embark on a
journey. A debt to my father I must repay
through the solace found in the practice of
serenity. Each bead on my mala, a silent prayer,
a bridge between our worlds.

Antara Unleashed -
Wicked Witch of the East

One morning, Antara wakes from a dream to realise her goddesshood. A beautiful black goddess, many-breasted, walks slowly across a bridge. She looks back at Antara over a gleaming ebony shoulder and, smiling, empties the golden goblet she carries into the waters below. Her limbs shatter. She emerges, a white goddess. Antara seeks feverishly for the meaning of the dream-vision. She rushes to Mr. Brown, the Tarot reader, a short, balding man with hypnotic green eyes. Antara loves to watch the cards turn up; the anticipation is addictive, as is the ambience. Dark room, black tablecloth on the round table. Books on the Tarot and other occult subjects. Sandalwood incense; a large crystal ball covered in black, which he unveils, into which he peers. Aliester Crowley could have looked like Mr. Brown. He reminds her of Crowley. She had felt a pang of delicious fear when he had asked her once, "Have you ever felt a male spirit force by your bedside, trying to caress you and lie on top of you?" Antara had thought, an incubus, a demon lover! Could it be Mr. Brown himself, trying out the sinister tricks he had mastered on his travels abroad? He claimed to be a warlock. He told her they plunged a knife into his heart during initiation, and he survived without a scar, yet there had been blood spurting from him like a fountain.

"You will believe what you want to believe,"
Antara had said. "The truth has nothing to do
with it. Is it a spirit force you speak of, or a
dream, or just fantasy?"
"My dear," he said, green eyes piercing hers
across the table littered with books, "I am
speaking about astral bodies who want to
experience the human, which is far richer than
their own!"

Mr. Brown tells her the goblet she has seen in
her dream- vision is the Ace of Cups. She has
seen the Muse. Isis calling to her from her
ancient form—the many-breasted black Moon
Goddess. She has been the High Priestess of Isis
in a previous life in ancient Egypt.

Antara returns home in a daze. She searches for
the many-breasted Black Isis in books and
comes upon the ancient form of the Moon
Goddess, Diana of Ephesus. Her path is set. She
will invoke Isis, transform herself into the
goddess every night of the full moon. She will
create a small altar for Her. She will dress in a
thin blue gown during her rituals; blue, Her
sacred colour. She will beseech the Goddess for
beauty, for creativity, for her own Osiris, a love
that transcends the boundaries of life and death.
In the womb's hushed chamber, a love bloomed.

Isis, entwined with her brother Osiris, shared heartbeat their lullaby. Fate, a cruel jester, snatched him away. Set, his heart a venomous pit, tore Osiris limb from limb, scattering him across the Earth. Isis, draped in the cloak of mourning, embarked on a pilgrimage. With a heart that echoed the emptiness of a starless night, she traversed the world, each step a prayer whispered on the wind. Each fragment of Osiris, a shard of their fractured love, She gathered to resurrect. The blackness that clung to her wasn't just the colour of mourning, but the absence of his light.

Antara raises her arms to the goddess when she glimpses Her in the heavens. Sometimes she is out on the streets. People stop and stare. Her gang of friends and hangers-on are embarrassed, but she does not care. Magazines and newspapers call her the glamorous Wicked Witch of the East. She will create. She will create. Flowers will spring where she treads.

Necklace of Skulls

As the enraged Durga in battle
Bore Kali from her third eye
My mother bore me in her rage at sex
That destroyer of the young and free
In her angst at the stilling of her butterfly wings

From whence did it arise
This blue-black darkness
All conquering
When I was blinded
By the radiance of angel wings?
Yet…
Is the womb darkness to the unborn child?

I have filled my maw
With the Adoration of Men
Skulls on my Kali's Necklace
For you, my Mother
Have left it empty

My insatiable tongue
Lapped hungrily at their tears
The bloody sweat of their surrender
Their offerings of beating hearts
The tremors of their flailing thighs
And then my Kali's Necklace snapped
And the skulls
Of my Adorers
Bounced and cracked

Across the spaces of
My boundless vanity
Till I could no longer see them…
Or my vanity

I possess still
The nubile body of the adolescent
In my eyes
The clouds of my childhood
Still flit
Across an unfettered sky
For Kali destroys only to quicken
Rewriting Time itself

Antara Unleashed -
Broken China

And then sadness, a thief, steals the emerald
from his eyes. "Oh my baby, you have every
right to hate me! I've been the one to hurt you!"
"I'm not hurt." I try not to sound all choked up.
He hugs me, yet is stiff and brusque, sitting in a
chair, while I sit on his bed, my back against the
wall, as we watch David Lynch's brilliant
'Blue Velvet'.
"Why don't you sit here next to me?" I ask.
"Because my back doesn't feel good against the
wall." He has a slight curvature in the spine that
gives him severe backaches. I content myself
with a hand on his shoulder for a while. His
armpits are smelling a little. Perhaps it is the
reason for his not wanting closeness. How I
hope it is ! Watching the violated Nastasia
Kinski, who plays a pitiful, battered woman, I
feel self-pity well up in me. Her angelic lover
reminds me of how Florian used to be—at least
how I had always perceived him to be. He could
do no wrong. He could never hurt anyone, least
of all, me. But that was long ago. I feel like a
fool for having believed that about him. My
heart curls up and seems to die, and then flowers
again, fresh and young, when he tenderly tucks
me into bed, places his hand on my forehead,
closes his eyes, and says, "Sleep well, baby.
Tomorrow I drive you to Maastricht."

It is a four-hour drive to Maastricht from
Bochum. Florian is pale, his face tight and
ungiving, the litter of candy wrappers still upon
the seats. Just like the turmoil inside him. He
keeps the window slightly down to blow out his
cigarette smoke. The chilly air cuts me to the
skin. I snuggle deeper into my long fawn suede
coat with its soft collar of fake fur and look out
at the meadows brittle with a layer of frost.

I am beginning to wonder whether this romantic
arctic wasteland that I had so hoped to melt is
just as we left it—frozen.

The main square in Maastricht. It is beautiful,
very cold. I thrust my hands quickly into my
bright pink fingerless woollen gloves that reach
down past my wrists. A few men and women
dressed in dull greys walk in and out of the pubs
lining one side of the great square.
Gaily-coloured feather boas flutter from open-air
stalls. I've always wanted a feather boa.

My heels sink into the cracks between the
cobblestones. I pull them out hastily. I hate to
appear gauche.

Above me, upon a high pedestal stands a statue
of a male figure, dark and robed, holding aloft a

flaming torch. Fire in the moist, foggy
afternoon. Catching my wondering glance,
Florian, hauling out my suitcase, nose and ears
red with the cold, says, "It's called the Spirit of
Maastricht. That flame never goes out."

I do not know whether to feel sad or happy. Is
our flame about to go out, never to spark again?

We clatter across the square, down a narrow
alley, looking for The India House restaurant
above which my friend Jill lives. It is surreal.
Her address in her letters to me had read:
'Above India House', and now I am here.
We stop next to the restaurant, and Florian rings
the doorbell. I haven't seen Jill for six years. My
heart races. Is she as pretty as before? Has she
lost weight? What will she think of Florian?

Florian stands away from the door as though he
wants to disappear. It must be trying for him,
appearing the villainous lover who banished his
'great love' after she crossed oceans for him.

The door opens. Jill, a little plumper than before,
her shoulder-length hair as curly and blonde as
before, her eyes as blue, takes me into her arms,
gasping, "Antara!"

We kiss, we stare at each other, broad grins on
our faces, Florian forgotten. She wears black
tights with knee-high boots and a dark
 green dress.
"Let me look at you!" She holds me away from
her. "Pretty as ever. I like the coat." Then she
wrenches herself away from me, smiles coldly at
Florian. Jill can be an ice maiden when the
mood takes her. He shakes her hand and greets
her in German. Taking my luggage from me, she
leads us up three flights of carpeted stairs. I pity
Florian carrying my heavy suitcase with his bad
back.
"Sorry, Antara, my apartment is small and not
very tidy." Jill ushers us into her room.

Purple silk *saris* with gold borders curtain the
windows from ceiling to carpeted floor. Against
one wall stands a couch covered in purple velvet
and plump brocade cushions. A tall, slim, royal
blue vase with magenta plumes and wine rushes
decorates a round glass-topped table. A couple
of steps away, the gold head of Nefertiti with
that long, slender neck stares down at us from
atop a white cupboard. A strange female torso
sculpted from wire leans against the built-in
closet near the door. Jill's ebullience and wacky
artistic taste are everywhere. I want a room like
hers.

Florian dumps my suitcase near the couch and sits down on one of the elegant, high-backed chairs at the table. He looks tense. The corners of his green eyes seem to droop some more. I flop down onto the soft couch.

"Make yourselves comfortable," says Jill. "I'll get some tea. My finest China for you." She goes out the door.

"Ach, now I can relax. She really loves you," says Florian, a tremor in his voice, and he goes after her.

I want to weep, and yet I am too excited to weep. If only I could hear what they are saying to each other in the kitchen. Perhaps she is chiding him, and he is telling her to take care of me. I know, no matter what I say about Florian, Jill will hate him.

After five minutes, during which I examine the pack of tarot cards on the table and wonder about my future, they come back in. Florian looks like he is about to cry. His lips are trembling, his eyes too bright. Jill places a silver tray on the table and begins to pour the tea into exquisite tea cups.

"I'd better go," says Florian. "I have a long drive
back." He looks at me, a deep sadness in his
eyes, and shakes his head in that familiar way
that means he wants to comfort me. I rise from
the couch and put my arms around him. We hold
each other. I feel tears stinging my eyes. He is
shaking. Then his arms are no longer around me,
and with a tremulous, "Take care," he is gone.

I am glad my tears did not spill onto my cheeks.
I swallow the hurt and sit down in the chair he
had sat in, still warm from his body. Jill stirs the
tea in my cup, eyes averted.
"So that's that," I say.
"Drink," she says.
"What was he telling you?"
"That he was sorry he could not look after you.
That he feels guilty. He is depressed. I can tell.
Oh, the cruelty of it all! How could he? You've
travelled such a long way. He must have a pea
brain to invite you at this time."

I sip the mild Darjeeling tea, enjoying the feel of
the delicate porcelain in my hands. "Depressed?
Still? He told me his depression was over. Now I
know why his car is littered with candy
wrappers and he rejects what he adores. I wanted
to see him on my birthday, Jill. Two birthdays
without him. I had to learn my lesson. Sensei

told me I must transcend my desire, and now I
have the chance to. He has helped me. He really
has."

"I don't know. I really don't. How can you be
expected to stop feeling sexy? I can understand
being vegetarian—I still am, you know, although
it's so difficult here, everyone laughs at me. But
sex? It's natural when you love someone."
"Even when you don't love someone," I laugh.
And we both laugh like we always have. Outside
the windows curtained with purple silk saris, it
begins to snow.

City of Victory

Moonlight spills through the filigreed windows of the royal harem, painting silver stripes on the lovely face of Jehaan huddling beneath a tapestry woven with forgotten stories, the scent of rosewater clinging to its threads like a fading memory. The sandalwood paste smeared on the burning bare limbs of the women mingles its cool fragrance with roses and heady jasmine. Even the rain, a relentless drummer on the roof, cannot drown the yearning in her heart. Even blades of grass can inflict wounds.

Here, beauty is a currency—a gilded cage. Emeralds steal the night from her eyes, their weight a constant reminder of her captivity. The queen's touch, cool and assessing, sends shivers down her spine. She longs for the wind-whipped freedom of the unadorned desert.

In the growing twilight, the masses of rock become shadows, paving the earth, piercing the sky. It is impossible to tell rock-hewn temples from the twisting, gyrating shapes of stone. Their harmony disturbs her. Bleak, desolate, alone, they stretch into the arid distance. The guarding fingers of watchtowers manned by eunuchs mock Jehaan with promises of freedom just out of her reach.

Above her, the roof of the Lotus Mahal mimics lotus petals, a cruel reminder of a life beyond these walls. This morning, a dove, a fragile emblem of hope, met its demise on the iron spikes that trap her dreams.

Grief propels her onto Benwa's back. A desperate ride to the marketplace, a kaleidoscope of colours that momentarily drown the suffocating grays. No other market in the world is like it, overflowing with an extravagance of diamonds, rubies and emeralds as big as nuggets, flashing with gilded palanquins. No, not even the grandeur of Rome can parallel the solid gold walls of the royal palaces, studded with gems, the ornate beds of silver, the revelry of Vijayanagar's richly dressed inhabitants. Oranges, pomegranates, grapes, and roses fling their mellow scent everywhere. Yet, their sweetness cannot mask the bitter truth—she is imprisoned by sumptuousness. She dreams of tattered tents and goat cheese.Then, eyes—dark pools flecked with green—pierce through the chaos, igniting a spark in the deepest well of her being. A yearning, sharp and primal, takes root. The masked stranger, a figment of her imagination or a desert wind's whisper?

The Nine Nights of Dussehra. The City of Victory pulses with feverish heartbeat in the velvet nights. Fireworks bleed crimson and gold across the sky, raining down sparks on a carpet of roses. Elephants, armoured behemoths, trumpet their defiance, carrying castles of gilded dreams on their backs. Music, a serpent uncoiling, writhes through the air, weaving between the tinkling melody of golden anklets on dancing girls. The king, a bejewelled idol on an opulent throne, surveys his kingdom of vibrant excess. The sacred rituals begin. The blue shroud of incense smoke ascends, carrying the chanting of prayers, the rhythmic sound of drums. Torches flare everywhere. The rich, dark blood of sacrificial bulls bubbles and steams into the night.

Slowly, gracefully, weighed down by their heavy ornaments, the king's 12,000 wives and the harem of 700 princesses move in a glittering procession, followed by handmaidens bearing glowing lamps of gold. Jehaan, a captive star, feels the weight of a thousand eyes yet searches for a green gaze. Could this chaos be her escape? A sudden surge of rebellion propels her forward, a desperate search for a way out.

The stables, a haven of familiar scents, offer temporary solace. Benwa, her loyal companion, whinnies a soft welcome. Then, a flicker in the distance—a caravan, a lifeline winding through the jewelled madness. Hope, a wild bird, takes flight in her chest. At the entrance, a figure appears—a masked stranger, green eyes burning in the twilight. A gypsy, a reflection of her own yearning spirit! Benwa, usually placid, rears and whinnies. Jehaan, heart hammering a frantic rhythm, strokes the horse's velvet muzzle and asks, "Why do you mask yourself?"
"I am not what I seem, my lady," he says softly. "I am Mystery. You created me with
 your longing."
"You… you are not real then?"
"As real as your longing is."
She is puzzled, excited, afraid. Through the windows, she sees the caravan winding into the distance, bright with fireworks. No one notices the figure shrouded in the mantle on horseback as it gallops to mingle with the caravan.
Or the masked man following with the speed of the wind.

Blind Among Flowers

I am not blind.

It's only that I must wrap myself in these great
wings and hide.

Night has no existence for me. Solitary, I stand
upon this high cliff. Passing strangers assume I
am a creature born of the rock. Sometimes,
through my sheer black wings, I discern the
bright blurs of a thousand lamps burning at my
feet. They keep them alight night after night. I
can but imagine the beauty that surrounds me in
this eternal night. I wait for the time when they
will forget to keep the fires burning in the
crevices of rock. Then... ah, then I shall unfurl
these dead wings and soar.

 I'll tell you why they imprison me, why I stand
as still as the stone beneath my feet. It is my
philosophy they fear. Modesty, humility,
mediocrity— to them, these are admirable. Not
for them the virtues of nobility and unmarred
truth. In their eyes I'm fearsome to behold,
towering, black as night. My eyes are empty
slits. They cannot see my wings of gold, my fair
angelic form. I embody Truth, a principle that
eclipses mere modesty. The two cannot coexist.
Had I not spoken of the wonders I bring, they
might have worshipped me. But tell me, what is

the difference between proclaiming the truth
and harbouring it in silence? Show me a
talented soul unaware of their gift. Man thrives
on the knowledge of his own worth, a priceless
possession. This, the very essence of my
message, has branded me an outcast,
a grotesque anomaly.

But they will not have my tears.
Hark! The heavens open, a torrent of rain
extinguishes the lamps one by one. Villagers
scramble, their panicked cries echoing through
the valley. The long-awaited moment has
arrived. Behold! I unfurl my wings. They
cower, their faces obscured. I have no eyes for
them. The moon bathes the world in a silver
glow, flowers unfurl their petals in silent
symphony. Where I land matters not. Freedom is
all that matters. The night hums with the silken
whisper of my wings.

A gentle descent onto the verdant carpet of a
hidden forest. The rain has ceased. I venture
towards a hamlet nestled amongst the trees,
searching for a kindred spirit, a soul who
embraces Truth as the ultimate virtue. Curtained
windows, a faint, yearning light struggling to
break free. Doors shut against the alien embrace
of the night. I glide silently, eavesdropping on

hushed conversations. My heart grows heavy.
No whispers of beauty, no celebration of self.
One window is different. The drapes are drawn,
yet light spills through, painting streaks of silver
across the leaves. Voices— one harsh, the other
soft, masking disdain like a velvet-gloved claw.
"You are the most beautiful woman in the world,
Fairaslily. That's why you reject all suitors."
"We have nothing in common. And why should I
deny my beauty? Is it a crime to revel in who
 I am? There is a man out there, I know it, a man
who will mirror my ideals."
"Ideals! A house of cards built to be shattered.
Face reality, child. Modesty speaks louder than
arrogance."
"My ideals will remain my compass until my
final breath, Mother. You too are beautiful, yet
you deny it."
The mother's voice softens. "Because, daughter,
I wouldn't want to burden the less fortunate with
the truth."
"Don't they already know, Mother?"
"Perhaps, but I would rather not incite their
hatred."
"Let them hate. In their hearts, they confess. Pity
not those who refuse to see."
Her words spark a flicker of hope. Could this be
my kindred spirit?

"Sleep now, Mother. The moon is full, and I
yearn for a breath of fresh air."

My heart quickens as I hide among the
blossoming jasmine. The door creaks open,
revealing a vision, the most beautiful woman I
have ever encountered. Truth radiates from her
face, lending grace to her slender form. Her
melodious song fills the air as she gathers the
fragrant jasmine.
A wave of warmth washes over me. "Your voice
is as beautiful as you, Fairaslily."
She takes a hesitant step forward, the blossoms
scattering around her feet. "Who... what are
you?"

Here, under the watchful gaze of the moon, with
the scent of jasmine heavy in the air, I stand
poised to reveal myself. "I am Veritas," I rumble,
the word echoing through the stillness.
Fairaslily's breath catches in her throat.
Tentatively, she reaches towards me, moonlight
glinting off a silver ring adorned with a tiny
carved owl on her hand. "May I… may I
see you?"
Revealing myself in my entirety could be
overwhelming, even terrifying, for a human. But
to build trust, to forge a true connection, a
measure of vulnerability is necessary. With a

deep breath, I unfurl. Shimmering threads of gold weave through my wings, catching the moonlight, casting an ethereal glow. Fairaslily gasps. Awe battles with fear in her eyes, but a hint of a smile tugs at the corner of her lips. "They were right," she whispers. "You are… frightening and more beautiful than anything I could imagine." The tremor in her voice isn't solely of fear. It is laced with the thrill of serendipity. In that moment, under the watchful gaze of the moon, a silent understanding blooms between us.

Together, perhaps we can show the world the beauty that lies within Truth, the strength it offers and the freedom it grants. Together, we could rewrite the narrative, one truth at a time.

Kali's Lament - Part 1 -
The *Swayamvara*

I have been watching and waiting.
Loving Damayanti's loveliness
From the abyss of my nothingness.
Swans with wings of gold
Carry messages of love between
Damayanti and her Nala.
I have always been ugly.
How then expect the delicate lotus-eyed beauty
Slender waisted maiden to desire me?
I am Darkness to her Light.
And Nala, he is the glorious sun itself.
I wait. I wait. I wait.

Damayanti chooses Nala above men
Above the immortals.
She could have chosen me at her *swayamwara*.
But I was too late.
Indra, Varuna, Agni and Yama laughed at my
Late coming.
Yet in the guise of Nala
They could not deceive Damayanti.
She prayed for insight.
She saw one of the five Nalas cast a shadow.
His eyelids moved.
Drops of moisture stood on his skin.
His garments were dusty.
His garland beginning to fade.
His feet touched the earth.

Damayanti has beauty enough to lure the gods.
Indra sent her a garland of his precious
Parijata flowers.
Those sad flowers with hearts of orange
That spring from golden branches.
Those flowers that bloom in the twilight
Filling the air with their intoxicating fragrance
Only to perish at daybreak like love
Those flowers that grew
From the sad ashes of Parijata
Spurned by the sun.
Those flowers grace the wedding of
Nala and Damayanti.
Agni has given grace to Nala.
So he may behold the gods in the sacrificial fire.
Even the hard-as-stone God of Death Yama
Has bestowed upon him his culinary skills
His steadfastness in virtue.
Varuna gives Nala power over the waters.
But none give Nala immunity to my Evil.
None.
Had I been the Chosen One
Damayanti would sit beside me
On my throne of iron in subterranean splendour.
Had she chosen me, I would have chosen
None else.
I wait. I wait. I watch.
Damayanti's beauty is supernatural in its power.
Her skin is moonlight.

Her breasts are round and firm.
But I have no hands.
Her soul is unblemished.
Pale. Uninteresting.
How will I taint it?
I wait. I wait. I wait.

I shall send the faithful Dwapara
To spy on the doomed couple
So oblivious in their new-found joy.
They call me Evil, these mortals.
Yet their thoughts have borne me.
They bring the Kaliyuga upon themselves.

Kali's Lament - Part 2 - The Possession

Twelve cursed years have passed
Since the wedding.
Twelve long years.
An eternity, even to an immortal like me.
How happy they have been with each other!
Cooing like pigeons in shadowy groves.
While I burn, burn, burn.
Children have been born to them
Indrasena and Indrasen.
Indra's Parijata flowers.
But now I possess Nala.
Yet I cannot possess Damayanti.
She notices the change in Nala.
She shies from his touch.
My touch.
She asks why his touch is so cold.
For my hands that become hands only through
Nala are cold as ice.
How beautiful she is.
The years have not touched her skin
The innocence in her eyes.
I burn, burn, burn.
I have no hands.
But this is the beginning of Nala's end.

Nala sits down to pray with feet unwashed.
I enter through his mouth, choking his prayers.
Yet she fawns on him still, weak woman
Waits on him like a servant maid.
She loves him even now when at my urging
He gambles his kingdom
His treasures away in a game of dice with his
Brother, Pushkara.
This saccharine symphony of love
Sickens me, Damayanti.
These whispers of devotion
These promises painted in the
Colours of the dawn
They reek of a fleeting warmth
A firefly's glow in the face of the eternal night.
My night. My eternal night.

Yes, it was I that incited Pushkara
To challenge Nala.
I tell him he will win Nishadha's throne,
Treasures, all.
He is startled by my voice.
He looks wildly about.
But I have no face.
Nala's face is now my face.
"Who promises, who speaks?"
"I, Kali, Spirit of the Kaliyuga
That men like you have
Brought upon themselves."

Pushkara tries not to let his fear show
But he is pale like ashes from a funeral pyre.
"Spirit!" he cries, "do not go away
Fulfill your promises!"
"Very well," I tell him
Challenge your brother Nala to a game of dice.
Tell him his kingdom depends on it."
"And I shall win, you say.
But why?
Why do you plot Nala's ruin so relentlessly?
What good will it do you?"
"That I shall not reveal," I say.
"Be thankful that I would make you
King in his stead."
Pushkara believes he has come upon
Sudden powers.
He is greedy.
"Come play with me, brother," he says to Nala,
"At the Cows and Bull."
I watch, laughing.
Nala mumbles that he does not play dice.
Then he sees Damayanti, wringing nervously
The *pallav* of her *sari*.
And to prove he is a man,
A man not afraid of a challenge
He hisses fiercely
"Pushkara, I will play!"
How weak men become in proving themselves.
I command Dwapara to enter the dice.

They fall at Pushkara's will.
Nala plays with vigour, his jaw
Set in a stubborn line.
He stakes his gems.
He loses them.
He stakes his armlets, his ornate belt
Studded with emeralds
His necklaces of diamonds and rubies.
He loses them.
He stakes all the gold from his treasury.
The chariots drawn by his beloved horses
Even his royal robes
He loses them all.
I laugh.

Damayanti, my poor, helpless Damayanti
Falls at Nala's feet.
She pleads with him to stop, she weeps.
But he is cold.
Once upon a time
He could not bear to see her tears.
She recoils from him as though from a serpent.
As though from my ugliness.
Shouts outside the great palace doors.
The ministers, along with the whole of Nishadha
Have come to plead with their King.
News of his sudden weakness has spread
Like a river in flood.
Damayanti, her fair face stained with futile tears

Walks to the balcony
Her lovely shoulders drooping
To listen to her people.
She returns to Nala's side
Her steps soft, her voice soft.
"King, husband! The people are at the gates.
They wish to speak with you.
Will you see them?"
He does not look at her.
His eyes are on the dice.
He rolls them between his palms, eyes glittering.
"Either I lose all now," he thinks,
"Or I gain all I have lost."
He knows not I am within him
Listening to his every thought
Sensing as he senses
Touching as he touches.
Many days have gone by.
They play still.
Nala loses still.
Damayanti wonders still
At the transformed Nala.
She is not without womanly wiles.
She asks Vrihatsena to summon
A council of ministers.
Nala wishes to take stock of what is
Left in his treasury.
Almost all is lost.
"We too shall perish!" they cry.

Once again they ask for an audience
With their King.
Once again he says not a word.
Damayanti does not give up.
She speaks to Vrishni, Nala's friend
And charioteer.
Dwapara tells me she suspects her virtuous,
Just lord
Is under an evil spell.
He is no longer himself.
She commands Vrishni to take
The children to Vidarbha
To her royal father's palace.
She sees doom approaching
Dark winged.

But Vrishni has not returned from Vidarbha.
Sore at heart about his dear friend's
Evil metamorphosis
Hopeless about the future of Nishadha
He has chosen to become charioteer
To King Rituparna.

Nala, you have lost your only true friend.
In sorrow, he has abandoned you.
Guilt eats into his soul.
But he too sees your doom
Dark wings beating closer every hour.

Pushkara's greed makes his face radiant.
Nala loses still.
Damayanti wets Nala's feet with her hot tears.
He ignores her.
She believes he has ceased to love her.
Yet she hopes like all women hope.
She hopes he returns to his true self.
She sends her ministers to hunt
For practitioners of dark magic.
She prays all day.
But Nala ignores her.
The Dice consumes him.
His shame consumes him.
The magic cannot touch me.

Kali's Lament - Part 3 - Exile

Nala has lost it all at last.
Pushkara mocks him.
"One more throw! Just one more, brother.
Yet what can you stake now?
Nothing is left to you but Damayanti.
Shall we play for Damayanti, noble brother ?"
Nala does not answer.
It begins to dawn on him that he has lost
everything.
Nothing may he call his own.
Save the lovely, faithful Damayanti.
Why did he not heed her words?
Why did he not listen to his people?
What made him do it?
He cannot understand the stranger he has
become.
"I am not the man I used to be
But whoever I may be,
I am not going to stake Damayanti on the Dice."
He runs his fingers, now shorn of gems
Through his long, tangled hair.
He frowns at Pushkara.
Do brothers behave like he does?

Unconsciously, he gropes for the missing pearls
at his throat.
He looks down at the white silk dhoti he wears
He looks down at his sandals.
They are all he has left.
Besides Damayanti.
"Stake her too, you fool," I insist
"Where will you go now with her beside you?
She is an added burden.
You cannot feed yourself.
How feed her?
Let Pushkara keep her too and leave Nishadha!"
But he resists me.
He rubs his furrowed forehead
As though he seeks to erase these
Thoughts that are my thoughts.
He wonders, what makes him think this way
About his Damayanti
Mother of his children, loyal, gentle Damayanti
Loved even by the immortals.
She too, bereft of her jewels.
How can he deprive her of his love?
She is right to deny him the love of her body
For his touch is cold as ice
His heart is cold as ice
Pushkara gloats.
He looks about him at the richness of the palace
He rushes to the great windows and looks out
Upon the land.

"Mine!" he shouts, clasping his brother's gems
Around his throat
His fingers heavy with rings.
Stones, mere stones!
They shine, and mortals believe them precious.
They kill their kin for stones.
The people wail outside.
They beat their breasts
Tear their hair as though in mourning for
A King who is dead.
Nala, poor fool, walks through this noisy crowd
Eyes down, the sobbing Damayanti behind him.
And Pushkara, the gloating Pushkara
Shouts from the steps of Nala's palace
"Whoever gives help, food or
Shelter to Nala dies!
Let my will be known throughout the land.
I am henceforth King in Nishadha!"
The wailing ceases.
Fear replaces sorrow.
They dare not follow Nala and his queen
Proceeding through the gates
Like punished children.
Vengeance is mine!
Did the people not sing the praises of
Nala and Damayanti
For twelve long years?
Did Nala not make them a prosperous people?
Now, at pain of death, they cower in terror

And abandon their King.
My task is made easy.
Mortals are weak.
How easily they change their loyalties!

Kali's Lament - Part 4 - The Woods

Three nights Nala and Damayanti have lain
Outside the palace gates
Hoping for succour.
Lain in the dust that touched only
Their sandals once.
Now they grovel in it, their faces
And bodies stained.
But Damayanti in her beauty shines still.
And he, whom the gods called the sun,
Look at him!
Faded like a flower wrenched from its roots.
He weeps, his face buried in
Damayanti's breasts.
Through the silk, I too feel her voluptuousness
And long for more.

He begs her forgiveness.
She smiles at him through her tears.
She tells him, "I have nothing to forgive you,
My Lord
You are the Nala I know and love.
I shall never leave you.
Let us go to Vidarbha to my people.
The children wait for us.

We shall be safe there."
"No," says he, "No, we cannot go to Vidarbha.
You go, my beloved.
You are too delicate to lead a wanderer's life.
How can I appear before your people like this?
Look at me!
I plead with you, beloved, go on to Vidarbha
Leave me to my fate."
Ah, thinks he that it is his love speaking thus?
No, it is I.
But Damayanti will not hear of it.
She will not abandon him.
A lesser woman would have left his side for the
Comfort of her home, her children.
But Damayanti, she will do
Anything for her passion.
"Wait," she tells him, "they will come for us.
Varshneya will come.
She has nursed me.
She loves us both.
She is no coward."
But Varshneya comes not.

Hunger makes them weak.
They wander through the woods
Like spirits trapped on the Earth plane
By their maya.
Wild are their eyes.
Searching for food and drink.

They drink from pools, eat roots and berries.
But hunger gnaws at them still.
Damayanti's *sari* is muddy
Her knee-length hair in tangles.
But it is not enough.
They have not suffered enough.
I speak to Dwapara of ways to further
Their downfall.

"Look Damayanti," cries Nala
"Look at those birds with wings of gold.
Today we shall eat well!"
He unwinds the white silk dhoti from his waist.
Lightly, he flings it upon the
Flock of shining swans.
He has a fondness for the birds that bore
Messages of his love to Damayanti.
The laugh dies on his lips as
Dwapara takes to the air
His many wings of gold
Bearing the garment aloft.
"You are sick to your brains, Prince!"
Dwapara cries
Hovering above the bewildered Nala
Now naked except for a loincloth.
"We are the Dice.
We came to take from you your last garment
You shall leave Nishadha owning nothing!"
Damayanti sinks to the ground

Not heeding the thorns piercing her knees.
Nala stands, staring at the garment flapping on
Wings of evil.
He cannot believe his ill fortune.
What has he done to deserve this?
It must be his karma.
He must have done something evil.
In a previous life.
The Dice had been possessed, but by what?
Is he possessed too?
Did not strange thoughts spring to
His mind unbidden?
His features contort with fear.
How did it happen?
He had always been clean in body
Dutifully performing the sacrifices to the gods.
He had been a good, just ruler.
He casts his mind back to that day of the Dice.
O folly most vile!
Had he forgotten to wash before
Sitting down to pray?
He touches the mute Damayanti.
Mute, but how she curses the Spirit of the Dice!
I feel her anger, tearing, tearing, tearing.
"O blameless one, they who have
Driven me away with their malice
They who bade my brother
Order our people to abandon us
They who starve us in this wilderness

They, Demon and Dice
Have taken from me my last garment!
Such shame have I fallen to
Such sorrow, wretched, demented
I am your Lord still, and I give you good advice.
Listen to me, beloved.
From here there are many roads.
That southwards go.
Some pass Avanti's walls
Some skirt Rikshavan, the Forest of Bears
This one leads to Vindhya's lofty peaks
This to those green banks
Where the fast-flowing Payoshni
Runs seaward through
Hermitages rich in fruit and roots.
And there, that path leads to Vidarbha
Where our children wait."
Foolish daughter of Bhima.
She should heed Nala's advice.
It satisfies me that she ignores it.
Her head bowed with grief
Her voice choked with sobs
Softly, she says, "Hunger makes me weak, Lord
Yet your words weaken me further.
Robbed of your realms
Stripped of your wealth
Naked, starving
Parched with thirst as you are
How shall I leave you in these

Untrodden woods?
While you dream of the good days past
I, in this wild place, shall
Charm your sorrows away.
I shall comfort you.
The wisest doctors say, 'In every woe
No better physic than wifely love'.
Nala, I will prove to you that this is true!"
"It is true," says Nala,stroking her dusty hair
"My sweet Damayanti, there is no friend
To a sad man except his own wife.
I would not even dream of leaving you,
My foolish beloved.
Why do you fear it?
It is rather from myself that I would flee
Not from you, you who are faultless."
"Why then, if you think not of leaving me
Do you point to Vidarbha's walls?
I know you will not leave me, Lord.
Perhaps you said it because
You are so without hope.
Do not look towards the south
Do not will me to leave!
Let us go there together, hand in hand.
You will be honoured by my father
We will be happy there with the children...
Happy and safe!"
She holds his hands, eyes beseeching.
"Never! Whatever happens, I shall not go there.

I went there glorious to make you my bride.
How can I return now,
Scorned and shamed thus?"
"It is his pride," she tells herself.
Yes, her thoughts too, I hear.
Am I not omnipotent?
Pride is my greatest virtue.
I admire Nala for his pride.
For without pride, what am I
But the abyss without end
A hollow pantomime of 'Evil'?

In silence, they wander through the undergrowth
Steps dragging
Damayanti's silken yellow *pallav*
Captured and torn by the briars.
A hut they spy through the dancing leaves.
The door hangs gaping like a wound
From a half-eaten hinge.
The cool, smooth mud floor comforts her feet.
Broken boards on the windows.
Red light of the dying sun
Caresses them with guilty fingers
They sink silently to the floor
In restless slumber.

Kali's Lament - Part 5 - Abandonment

Within the crumbling hut in the woods
Nala wakes.
Touches softly the withered white roses
In Damayanti's tangled hair.
She does not belong here with him.
He does not deserve her, the wretch.
Her sandals are torn.
Thorns embedded in the tender
Flesh of her lovely feet.
He draws them out, bloody tipped
As gently as he can.
Why is he so afraid to wake her?
Does he mean to abandon her to the mercy of
The cruel woods
The sly night?
Yet how fondly she shares his fate!
Yes, abandon her to her destiny.
The woods will not swallow her.
The very leaves of the trees shall protect her,
The very earth on which she treads
With faltering steps.
Is she not radiant?
So full of grace
Her every movement a dancing?

Is she not noble, faithful, pure?
But how can he leave
Naked from her side?
He reaches towards her again
Thinking to rend a piece of her *pallav*.
He draws back.
Will she not be roused by it?
She will wake.
She will cling to him.
He rises.
Creeps along the walls in search of
Something sharp.
He finds it in a chink.
A gleaming knife, keen-edged.
Many a time he bends over her, knife poised.
Each time he draws back.
He is taking from her.
Offering nothing in return.
Damayanti moans.
Her eyelids flutter.
His heart beats miserably.
He waits till her moaning stems and then
Cautiously, lifts her dusty *pallav*
Cuts away a piece.
"I have severed our love with this knife."
He wraps the cloth around him
Steps out of the hut.
Shamed, he returns to peer at her through
The doorway.

How peacefully she sleeps
Consoled in the knowledge that
Her Lord is nearby.
In silence, he weeps.
"Ah, my love, whom neither wind nor sun
Has harshly touched
How unaware you are, how trusting!
Oh, my slender-waisted queen
With the bright smile
Will you not wake to madness?
And when you wander in the wild woods alone
How will you fare, Bhima's tender child?
My most noble wife
May the great sun
May the eight powers of air
The Rudras
The Maruts
The Aswins guard you
True and dear one
On your way home!
At last, driven by me
He flies from the slumbering Damayanti
Lost to love.
He flees through the woods
My soulless prey.

Damayanti wakes
Shuddering at the silence of the woods.
The great silence makes her eyelids flutter open.

Why cannot she hear her beloved's breath?
Her fingers reach towards the floor beside her.
Anguish seizes her.
"Maharaja!" she cries in a voice
Broken with tears.
"Why have you abandoned me?
Now I am lost.
How lonely it is, how silent!"
She hides her face in her torn *pallav.*
She weeps loudly.
Nala's love a flickering candle, Damayanti
Extinguished by the first gust of adversity.
Mine, Damayanti, is a raging inferno
A storm that consumes and refines.
Let the flames cleanse you
Burn away the remnants of betrayal
Forge you into something stronger
Something magnificent.
Love, they whisper
A fleeting thing
A moth drawn to a flickering flame.
Love, they sigh
A pathetic trick
A gilded cage for foolish hearts.

But Damayanti, oh Damayanti
Your defiance like a supernova burns.
Your eyes hold a different truth.
A fierce tenderness

A loyalty brighter than any divine spark.
It maddens me, this devotion
This strength that defies my knowing.
Is it a weapon
Wielded by the pure against the corrupt?
Or a weakness
A vulnerability I can exploit?
Perhaps it is both.
Perhaps love
This thing that repulses and intrigues me
Is the very chink in your armour
And I may yet unravel you.
For if I can twist love
Mould it into a weapon of despair
Surely your precious loyalty will crumble.
And in the wreckage
I will claim you
Not with desire
But with a cold, terrible understanding.

Kali's Lament - Part 6 - Dangers for Damayanti

Damayanti sees not the beauty about her
Nor senses the fragrance of the jasmine wild.
She hears not the peacock's cry.
She clasps her hands, she curses:
"Whoever has cast this evil spell upon my Lord
I pray he suffers a far bitter fate.
I pray his days are darker than yours, my Nala!"
You curse me, Damayanti, my love.
My only love!
Look upon me, and tremble!
My form, a tempest of shadows
A coiling vortex of primordial power.
My eyes
Twin infernos have witnessed the birth and
Death of countless stars.
My touch, the caress of a dying sun
A whisper of annihilation that chills
The marrow of gods themselves.
Do you see love, frail human
In this visage of absolute dominion?
Your curse cannot even graze
My obsidian cheek.
Screaming, she trips
horrified over a great serpent's coils.

Great, gleaming, powerful coils embrace her.
Yet even now she weeps for Nala
And her children
And not for herself.
"My children," she gasps
"Will your fingers ever clasp a father's hands?
Ah, Nala, my Love, you who would have
Saved me if you could
What will you do
When free from the evil spell
You regain all but your wife?
Who will look after you with love
When I lie dead?
Come to me now
Let me see you one last time!"
The forked tongue flickers over her
Shivering limbs.
Those foaming jaws gorge her body till her hips.
Her perfect breasts heave in panic.
"Help!" she shouts
Pity me, save me from this dreadful death!"
The vultures reel overhead.
But she is saved by a hunter
Wandering through the forest.
He rushes to her side
Marvelling at her loveliness.
He slices through the serpent with a single
Swift blow of his sword.
He lifts her from the dying, writhing coils.

He wipes the foam from her body
Fingers trembling with desire.
Seeing her hunger
He feeds her berries he has
Gathered in the forest.
He watches her closely
Watches the hunger die in her almond eyes.
But there is hunger in him now.
"What are you doing here in this wilderness,
Beautiful one?
How did you fall into the jaws of death?"
She tells him how her Lord and
King of Nishadha
Possessed by some evil spirit
Lost all in a game of dice with his
Avaricious brother.
The hunter does not listen to her words.
Lust rises in him as he gazes at
Her voluptuousness
Those long, dark lashes cast shadows
Upon her cheeks.
Her tender sighs, her honey-sweet voice
Sets him afire.
He puts his arms around the startled queen.
His lewd whispers hot upon her neck.
She flings him from her.
She burns, how she burns, a goddess insulted.
Her eyes blaze.
Her skin afire.

"If I am clear in heart and true to my Lord
Then may you
Vile murderer of innocent beasts
Fall to the earth, stone dead!"
And the hunter falls
Struck by the lightning blazing from her eyes
Shaking hands, clutching at his throat.
Flames flicker on the wind.
The hunter, a pile of ashes at her feet.
She stares at the ashes with horror
She whispers
"What former deeds of mine
Are the cause of all my travails?"

Kali's Lament - Part 7 - Prophecy

The forest reveals its true self to Damayanti
As she flees through the trees,
She knows not where.
It is evening.
The forest lonely, filled with shadows.
She hears the sound of beasts greeting
The oncoming night.
Lions, wolves, deer, bears, leopards.
Then the strident low trill of the crickets begins.
She thinks about those silver-belled anklets
She so loved to wear.
The trees are assuming the shape of truth.
The Semul tree is the goddess, Lakshmi
With arms outstretched.
Even in the dark
The bright red cup-like flowers
Sacred to Lord Shiva
Glow like drops of blood.
The Creator of the world, Pitamaha
Once rested after his labours
Beneath Semul branches.
How strange then that its thorns
Torture the unfortunate
In one of the seven hells!
Bird nests blanket the trees.

All this Damayanti beholds.
She sees the Creator resting beneath
The branches of the Semul.
She rushes towards Him, words about Nala
On her lips
But He is gone.
Fantastic images pass before her entranced eyes.
It is difficult to believe that she destroys
With a flash of her soul-filled eyes.
She walks on
Eyes darting in all directions
Sick for the sight of her Lord.
She feels her aloneness pressing upon her.
Who is there to shelter her
From the shadows in this wild place?
As though through a mist
She sees hideous shapes
Flitting through the trees.
A great wind
Begins to blow
Whipping her long hair into her eyes
Whistling past her unadorned ears.
"The rakshasa breathes!" she cries.
Dwapara sees the rakshasa too.
His breath is the wind
Mowing down the trees in its path
Bending Damayanti's slender waist
Like the stem of a flower.

She shields her eyes from the storm
Of leaves and dust.
She stares ahead.
She watches the giant turn into a
Gnarled old woman
In a shining robe, a deer, an eagle, a wolf.
She sees the *pishachas*
Flitting through the green air
Their feet turned backwards
Shrieking in nasal voices.
Serpents swing from the branches above her
Fierce bison paw the earth
Grey boars root for food.
The roar of waterfalls fills the forest.
Moonlight limns the shapes of
Beasts at the waterhole.
The sound gladdens her.
Peaks rise before her.
She glides towards a rock like a *pishacha*.
She lifts her face heavenwards and speaks:
"Nishadha's king, where have you gone
Leaving me alone in this uninhabited wood?
You gave your people numberless gifts
You performed the great *Aswamedha* Sacrifice
Who could offer more to the gods?
But what have you given me?
An empty vow!
The golden tiger draws near.
He stands squarely before her

Powerful paws planted on the earth
Like pillars with roots.
He pants, great wet pink tongue
Lolling drops of saliva.
She winces at the sight of his long yellow fangs.
She draws back two steps
Her *pallav* stretched to tearing point
Between her shaking fingers.
"Dreadful lord of this wilderness,"
She stares into his eyes.
"You are the king of beasts.
I am the daughter of Vidarbha's king, Bhima.
I am Nala's wife, Nala, Subduer of Foes.
I seek him here, alone and miserable.
Will you not offer me comfort?
If you have not seen Nala
Tear me to pieces, O savage lord
Devour me, set me free from my sorrow!"
The beast does not answer.
He turns his golden striped back on her.
Stalks down to the river that glitters
Through the reeds.
River seeking sea.
Three nights Damayanti
Passes in the wilderness.
She journeys northward and comes
Upon a silent green grove
Morning peace heavy upon the trees.
It is a hermitage, a ring of

Leaf huts.
Small fires dot the undergrowth.
Embers glow a pale red in the pale light.
A crystal stream meanders, singing
Through the flowering trees.
She sees the emaciated yogis sitting
cross-legged
Beneath the trees.
Eyes open, yet unseeing in meditation deep.
She recalls the ancient ones
Vasistha, Bhrigu and Attri
Who lived their lives eating sparsely
Taming their passions
Pure in heart
Breathing slow breaths
Seeking the heavenward road
Fearless wild creatures graze around this haunt
Monkeys, black-faced and curious,
Throng the trees.
She is glad to feel her tense muscles relax
Glad to be free of the beast-haunted night.
Here is a shelter of peace.
Yogis bury themselves alive for days
To emerge still breathing in the slow,
Imperceptible way of deep meditation.
They walk on water
They perform amazing feats.
But how long does it take them to learn?
Conquests of things trivial!

Yet these yogis speak of Evil.
They that torture themselves
Sacrifice their comforts
Renounce their loved ones
To bring suffering upon themselves!
They rise from their meditation.
They see Damayanti in her weary loveliness.
Jewelless, unadorned, she seems a queen.
With folded hands, they greet her.
"Welcome! Rest here for a while with us
Tell us what you would have us do."
"Worshipful ones who live in peace
In the midst of wild beasts
And hard work, is it well with you?"
"We thank you, noble lady; it is well with us.
Who are you, so beautiful,
So noble, yet so sorrowful?
Are you the mountain yakshi
Or the spirit that lives in the river?"
She smiles, "None of these am I
No goddess of the wood
Nor mountain or water sprite. I am a woman
with a tragic tale." She speaks about herself
Not a quaver of self-pity in her voice
Wearily, she asks, "Have you not seen my Nala?
If I do not find him now
I shall find peace only in death.
I cannot live without my Lord.
Why breathe when my soul is dead?"

"Beautiful one, the future is yours
It will be great, that we foresee.
We see your Lord before us.
You will see him soon.
Yes, you will regain your lost love,
Bhima's sad daughter!
You will know him as your Nala of times gone
Free from trouble, purged of sin
Governing all Nishadha again in his glory
Once again, the joy of his friends
And terror of his foes."
Damayanti means to thank them
For their comfort
But they vanish before her astonished eyes
Huts,
Fires,
Stream,
Grove,
All.
"Was it a dream?
Why has this happened to me? Illusions!
I am seeing things in my misery.
Where did they go?"
She sighs, "Illusions!" and moves on.
The spring is gone from her step
Her head hangs like a wilting flower.
She spies the Ashoka tree that takes away grief.
She flings herself upon the dark brown trunk.
There are no flowers.

If there were flowers
She would have soaked them in water
Drunk a palmful to soothe her sorrow.
"And flowers there shall be!" she cries
Touching the tree with her left foot.
Buds break upon the branches and open slowly
The soothing pale yellow flowers of the Ashoka.
Excited, she makes a container from a large,
Shiny leaf
Drops the flowers one by one into water culled
From a nearby spring.
Smiling, she stirs the potion with a finger
Then lifting it to her cracked
Dust-stained lips, drinks.
And claimed by sleep
Forgets her searing pain for the night
Like Sita fleeing from Ravana
She would lie safely beneath the Ashoka
No beast, no ghoul would venture
Into its shadow.
Even I, Kali
Shun it.

Kali's Lament - Part 8 -
The Elephant Stampede

Dwapara sees the caravan
Before Damayanti comes upon it.
She stops to rest on that long, weary road.
Barely has she caught her breath
When she starts as though from a dream
At the rolling,
Splashing,
Churning sounds of laden horses
Wading through the river to her left.
She laughs with relief.
She delights in the colours and textures
Of silk and muslin bales
On the backs of scornful, loping camels.
She longs for the feeling of
Clean silk on her limbs.
She frowns down at her rags.
She watches the elephants
Lumbering up the bank,
Their wet bellies gleaming.
There is a great clamour of
Neighing and trumpeting
The jingle of harnesses
And the hoarse shouts of the merchants.
Damayanti rushes to the bank

Dusty, long matted locks flying, thin and pale
She whose smile was once so beautiful
But they pass her by; they taunt her.
"What? Nowhere to go, pretty beggar maid?"
Yet one there is who dismounts
From his dark steed
"Enough!" he shouts at the men
In a powerful voice.
He looks long at the lovely, gasping Damayanti.
No beggar maid is she.
"Who are you, and how do you come into this
Wild place?" he asks
"Your appearance astonishes me.
Are you one of us or a
Spirit wild of river valley?
Tell me the truth.
If indeed you are a spirit
Grant us good fortune
And safety on our journey home."
She answers as before.
Once again, her eyes are alight with hope.
They throng around her now
Wondering at her noble speech.
Some seem ashamed.
"I am Suchi," says the merchant, "
Leader of this caravan.
Many are the places I have travelled
Yet never have I heard of this
King you speak of.

For a long while now
Travelling through this forest
We have not seen a human shape but yours.
May Manibhadra, Lord of Yakshas, honour me
As I speak the truth!"
Once again, the droop of her eyes, her body.
"Where are you going?" she asks.
"To Chedi, where the just Subahu is king
We go to sell our goods.
You are welcome to travel with us if you wish."
They camp near a wondrous deep pool
Where the lotus flowers.
The lotus eyes of Damayanti open wider.
All around the boughs are heavy
With fragrant blossoms
The grass rich
Petals drop into the water to float aimlessly
Until captured by lotus leaves
Bejewelled with trembling drops of rain.
Birds sing in this haven
Feasting on fruit no mortal has yet tasted
For this is a virgin place.
She rests on the grass
Dips her dusty feet into the
Cool water of the pool.
She laves her weary limbs
She drinks deep,
Breathes the scented air.
Peace comes to her,

Hope fills her soul to bursting.
Surrounded by such beauty, how can she remain
Stricken with grief?
She sees Nala in every
Flower and blade of grass.
She knows with unshakeable certainty
That he waits for her.
The men, weary, hungry-eyed,
Cast longing, curious glances at her.
She sits at a distance from them.
There is no space for sin here in this
Lovely place.
Suchi orders a tent for her beside the pool.
He sends her a meal of fresh honey and fruit.

She sleeps, my Damayanti, a restful sleep at last.
The night is deep.
Stars shine through the trees.
But sweet slumber is broken
Damayanti wakes to the
Sound of trumpeting and stamping.
The earth quivers under the
Berserk rush of elephants
Thirsting for the waters of the pool.
The mazda of madness
Oozes from their great heads.
The elephant cows tied to
Tree trunks trumpet in answer
Their gigantic legs wrinkled and grey

Pull at the ropes
The trees begin to sway.
Damayanti is the first to rise
She trembles at the looming dark shapes
As they bear down upon the camp
Breaking through thorny briars
Mowing down mighty trees
Uprooting rocks.
"Stop!" she cries, "Let me live,
I have yet to find my Nala!"
"The elephants, the mad elephants!"
Cry the merchants and their attendants
Running hither and thither
Only to be squashed like fruit in the stampede.
Blood and guts everywhere.
Some stare unbelieving as in a dream
Grasping at sleep
And are trampled among the flowers.
The horses and camels die gory deaths.
The elephant cows join the mad herd
Dragging splintered tree trunks behind them.
"No, not the horses, not the horses!" she screams
Agonised by their rolling eyes filled with terror
Convulsing bodies.
How Nala had loved horses!
There are voices now
"Fire in the tents! Fly for your lives!"
"Look where we leave our treasures
Trod upon by mad beasts!

Gather them!
Stop!
Why do you run away
Leaving your treasures behind?
Stop, I tell you, cowards!"
"Fly, fly for your lives!"
"We die!"
"O cowards!"
Damayanti cowers beneath her fallen tent
Barely breathing.
Their words sadden her.
"Why has this misfortune befallen us?
Whose evil curse is this?
Have we not worshipped mighty Manibhadra
And Vaishravan, King of Yakshas?
Have we not made offerings to
The spirits that impede?
Were the stars adverse?
Who is that woman with the insane eyes
That stole into our caravan?
Surely ill-favoured is she.
She seems barely mortal!
Surely she is the cause of this calamity.
Our goods, our friends gone!
She is an evil sorceress
Demon, witch or gliding ghost!
She has murdered us at midnight.
There is no doubt.
It is she!"

"Where is she?
If only we could spy her, our ruin
We would strike her dead with stones,
Canes and clubs
With our bare hands!"
Damayanti listens
Trembling, flees into the thicket, shamed,
Breathless, guilty.
"Perhaps they are right. I caused this.
Struck with ill fortune.
I bring calamity upon everyone I meet
Nala, did I bring misfortune to you too?
Am I truly good for you?
O Pitiless Fate!
Not a ray of light in my darkness.
What wrong have I done?
I cannot think of any
Whether in thought or deed.
Then why this curse?
Perhaps it is my karma
Punishment for the sins of a previous birth.
What was I in my previous life?
What sin was mine?
My palace lost,
My children, my husband too.
I am torn from my home
Ripped from my mother's womb!"
She thinks of me.
Is this the Evil One's doing?

Has he condemned me to forever grieve?
Those golden swans
That robbed Nala of his garment
Where are they now?"
The pain is great in me
Tearing through my darkness
"Oh beloved, does the Evil One
Plague you still?
Are you possessed by Him?"
Realisation dawns. "Ah, so it is.
My Lord, you were possessed
From the moment you threw the dice
That is why you seemed so changed!
How do I find you, beloved?
How do I free you from the spell?
You were flawless once
Like a stream running pure from the snows."
But Suchi, who knows Damayanti is innocent
As the cloud that has not rained
Lies dead.
Hiding from the eyes of the
Remaining merchants
Damayanti toils towards Chedi
On blistered feet.

Kali's Lament - Part 9 -
The Metamorphosis of Nala

Nala flies blinded through the forest
Pursued by his great guilt.
He knows not which is his true self
The one that says,
"You shouldn't have abandoned your wife!"
Or the one that says, "You did the right thing."
He runs
His feet seem to possess a will of their own.
He cannot arrest their maddened movement.
He smells smoke
He smells singed flesh and fur.
A wall of flames is suddenly before him
A furious blaze.
Boughs crash around him
The flames crackling
The heat
The smoke intense.
Animals flee from the lick of the flames
Their cries sound the alarm.
He feels fur brush against his legs
He hears an anguished voice.
"Oh Nala, turn your steps towards the fire
I burn, I die!"
"I come," he answers

"Take courage, whoever you are!"
He thinks, surely it is a friend's voice
Calling my name
But the fire rages
The trees are torches
The heat intense
And I,
Only human.
Yet he nears the blazing wall
Walks through it,
Eyes closed
Hands covering his head.
But what is this?
The flames are cool upon his skin.
Opening his wondering eyes
He sees Lord Agni before him
Red hair in flames.
"You forget, Nala," says Agni
"You forget I granted you immunity to fire
When you were a babe.
Do not be afraid!"
Dumbfounded, Nala watches the god
Melt into the flames
Before he forges triumphant
Through the burning bushes
Searching for the voice.

In a clearing covered with ash
He comes upon the Naga

God of the underworld.
His scaly hands folded in prayer.
Rubies glow red in his crown.
Thick black coils
Writhe from the waist downwards.
The Naga's skin blushes in the heat.
"I am Karkotaka, the one that
Betrayed the Sage Narada
And now I suffer from his curse.
He has imprisoned me on this very spot.
But you have come at last.
If you save me from the flames,
I shall regain my freedom.
O mighty Prince, save me now
I shall reward you a hundred times over.
I shall be your devoted servant for life.
I shall help you attain great happiness.
I know you search for your happiness!
Come hither, lift me from this accursed spot
You will not find me heavy."
The snake god shrinks to the length of a finger.
Nala carries the Naga away from the flames
Where the air is fresh.
"You may go now, kind King.
May good fortune accompany you,"
Says Karkotaka.
But scarcely has Nala taken nine steps
When he feels the serpent's fangs
Sink into his heel

With a sharp searing.
He gasps in astonishment.
He bends down to massage his heel.
Oh, how I burn!
Not even Damayanti's curses compare
With this searing suffocation!
Something is trying to push me out.
I must use all my strength to hold onto Nala.
I shall not leave him until he is destroyed
Until I possess Damayanti.
"What? Is this how you repay my favour?"
Nala stares down with horror at his limbs
"What have you done to me?"
His body is stunted
Misshapen
Grotesque.
The trees tower above his head.
"You have transformed me into an ugly dwarf!"
"So that no man will know you are Nala.
The Evil One within you shall suffer
Even greater agony than you do
At this moment.
He shall not find rest from my potent venom
Until he leaves your body.
Fear not; my venom shall not poison you,
O King without a kingdom.
On the contrary,
It will give you further powers.
Fear not the charge of the wild boar

Nor your enemies
Nor a Brahman or sage.
You will find victory in every battle you wage.
Go now with a new identity.
From now on, you are Vahuka, the Charioteer.
Hasten to the city of Ayodhya
Ask to serve as Raja Rituparna's charioteer.
He will teach you the secret of the dice
Of which he is a master.
You will teach him how to tame horses in return
An art of which you are master.
Your sorrows will end.
You will find your wife and children
You will rule Nishadha once more
You will win back your kingdom
Through the dice.
Here, take this enchanted robe.
When you wish to regain your true shape
Wear it and think of me."
Nala drapes the many coloured garment
Over his arm.
He rubs the gossamer fabric between his fingers.
The thinnest silk
Not woven by mortal hands.
"I knew you would not wish me ill,"
He says to the Naga
Karkotaka smiles.
And then he is gone
Vanished into the green.

How I detest you, snake vermin!
Your venom tortures me.
But it is not powerful enough to make me
Abandon Nala's body.
Nothing you can do shall make me
Give up Damayanti!
Vengeance is mine.
Nala is still under my spell.
I am his King.
I am his conscience.

Kali's Lament - Part 10 - Nala's Refuge

Ten days Nala journeys through the jungle
Appeasing his fierce hunger with
Wild fruit, herbs and roots.
Many a time he gazes at himself in still pools
And recoils from his ugliness.
He is both fascinated and repulsed by it.
He longs to wear the magic robe and
Watch himself grow
Whole and beautiful again
But he cannot call on the Naga
For the sake of his vanity.
His face! What has happened to his face?
What if Damayanti sees him thus?
Knowing the truth about his identity,
Would she love him still?
Does she love him still?
Lost and alone in the forest where
He had abandoned her!
She must hate him.
Has she encountered harm from man or beast?
Has she taken a new lover in revenge?
She is not to blame if she has.
He is a coward.

His thoughts fill the hours till he reaches
Ayodhya and seeks the court.

Uncertainty rages in him when he beholds
The fair Rituparna.
He notices the King wincing at his ugliness.
He sees the mockery on the faces of the court.
He sees the hidden smiles,
Hears the unsaid insults.
Gathering himself together,
Holding his head high, he speaks,
"I am Vahuka, the Charioteer, O King.
You will not find any other on Earth
Who has my skills in taming
And guiding horses
Or my skills in preparing meats
For the royal table.
I know it all.
Ugly am I,
Poison to the eyes
But I know it all.
Whatever the task you give me, big or small
I shall fulfill it, O King."
"I shall employ you, Vahuka as my
Charioteer and horse tamer
If you prove to me your skills.
Make my horses the swiftest in the land.
Can you do that?
Your wage shall be

Ten thousand gold sovereigns."
"Whatever you wish, my King,"
Nala bows his mangy head.
"You may stay then with my servants
Vrishni and Jivala.
They will acquaint you
With the horses and our customs."
Vrishni and Jivala, thinks Nala
They who looked after his horses in Nishadha!
They will never know him
Yet he is glad to see familiar faces.
Vrishni, his dearest friend.
The friend that abandoned him
With guilty heart!
He longs to tell Vrishni all,
Unburden himself.
Yet he must not.
The time has not come for that.
Nala has fine food, he has shelter
He has a goal, but his heart is never at rest.
He has not sweet Damayanti.
Every morning brings with it fresh longing.
Every evening he sits by himself
On the steps of his humble dwelling
Near which the stables smell of
Horse dung and sweat.
He sings one verse over and over again
"Where is she,
All weary,

Hungry and thirsty
Yet loyal as only she can be?
Does she think of me
Foolish man that abandoned her
In a moment of weakness?
Or is she, my beloved,
Wooed by another?"

Vrishni and Jivala wonder
At this daily refrain.
The song reminds Vrishni
Of something.
Did not his lord and mistress of days gone by
King Nala and his queen Damayanti
Wander through the forests
Banished from their own land?
Tears spring to his eyes at the memory.
He is moved by the dwarf's plight.
Where does he come from,
This horribly deformed creature?
Who is the fair maiden he sings of?
Is she as grotesque as he?
He chides himself for his careless thoughts.
Lovers, no matter how ugly
Are always beautiful to each other.
He tells the curious Jivala,
"Leave him be.
Whom he sings of is his own business.
If he wants to tell us about his tragedy,

He will."
But Jivala heeds not.
"For whom do you sorrow, O Vahuka?
Please tell me, I am your friend.
Who is the cursed husband of this
Unfortunate maiden?"
"I sing of a lady who was wedded to
A weak-willed man, my friend.
She is so beautiful, so virtuous
So loyal,
That no other could match her.
As they wandered together in the wilderness
He fled from her while she slept.
He believes he was not himself then
But possessed by something evil.
How could he have abandoned her
Left her to the mercy of beasts?
Racked by sorrow was he at this deed.
Today he sings this same sad song.
He is a lone traveller
World-weary, his sorrow is without end
He longs for her,
The Blameless One.
All alone and sad,
She must wander the jungle
Searching for him,
Always searching!
Perhaps she lives no longer.
The jungle is fraught with dangers."

Jivala places a hand on Nala's shoulder.
"You sing as though
You yourself have abandoned her, Vahuka–"
"Oh, it is I, it is I
That evil one who has abandoned
His only true love!"
Cries Nala uncontrollably
Grasping Jivala's hand.
"Listen to my counsel, friend.
You will find her
Perhaps I can help you find her
But sing not of her on our doorstep.
Let not the world into your secret.
They will pity you,
Laugh at you, friend
They will not understand."
Nala bursts to tell Jivala all.
Yet he does not name her.
It would be foolish to name her.
Jivala knows him
Yet knows him not.
Nala feels the well of his loneliness
Grow deeper still.

Kali's Lament - Part 11 - Damayanti Found

King Bhima's messenger
The twice-born Suhadeva has reached
King Subahu's court.
How will she,
The fair and beauteous secret one
Now conceal her identity?
Yet how will Suhadeva know one
So marked with grief?
Her lovely lips droop at the corners.
Her eyes seldom laugh
Even at the young Sunanda's jests.
This morning too, she asks if there is a Brahman
Come with news for her.
"None yet, my dear Urvashi,"
Answers Sunanda sadly.
Damayanti wanders into the gardens
Where the peacocks play
The blue lotus flowers.
"Ah, Nala, my beloved
I have no news of you
Not even today!"
Suhadeva hears her and wiping with haste
The tears that spring to his eyes
Approaches the sad, wilting form

Beside the fountain.
Has he heard right?
Did she call Nala's name?
Is it truly Damayanti
The most beautiful woman
In the three worlds?
Ah, but behold her eyes,
Lustreless
Yet long-lashed and lovely still.
Only Damayanti has those eyes!
And wait!
The mark between her brows!
Yes, it is she.
Ah lovely lotus bloom bruised by
The careless hand of Fate!
How dry are the pools of your almond eyes
All tears shed!
Ah, delicate Queen,
So tenderly reared to bloom in a palace
Built of precious gems
How you seem to wither here in this
Unknowing place
Rootless, dying.
Does Nala languish without you too
Living each day with hope
Or does he lose heart as the days go by
Without a sign from you?
I must bring you together
Not because King Bhima has promised me

A thousand bulls
A thousand acres of land
But because you are our Queen
Our flawless Queen.
He speaks over her shoulder:
"I have found you at last, O Queen.
Fear not, I am Suhadeva
Sent by your royal father
To bring you home to him."
Damayanti breathes deep
To still the thunder of her leaping heart.
"I thought you would never find me, Suhadeva!
Is my father well?
My children?"
"Yea, as well as they could be
Without you, my Queen.
They have no spirit without you."
"And Nala,
Surely you bring me news of Nala?"
"We seek him still.
A hundred twice-born rove the land
In his quest."
Damayanti weeps
Her tears mingle with the water in the fountain.
Her body is wracked with sobs.
"Weep not, Queen.
They will find Nala
As I have found you.
How pale,

How dim you have become in your grief!
Like the moon trying in vain
To shine through the mist."
Damayanti sighs.
"They speak the truth when they say
A husband is a woman's only ornament.
Without him
Even the world's most lustrous pearls
Round her throat seem dim."
Ah, contemptible mortals and their ways!
As though a human is nothing at all
Without another.
If so, what is he worth?

Sunanda has watched it all.
Watched with amazement Damayanti
Weep bitterly
Before a strange Brahman.
She turns with hurried steps toward
The palace doors.
"I knew it all along," says the Queen Mother.
Our noble guest was concealing
Something from us.
She is a princess born.
My blood does not deceive me.
Sunanda, daughter,
Summon them to me."

"I lied to you, Sunanda, dear friend.
How do I face you or the Queen Mother?"
Cries Damayanti
Blushing in her shame.
"Have no fear, Queen.
My mother is kind.
She likes you, you know that.
Come, she asks for you both.
Do you know whose wife
Whose daughter is this, O twice born?"
The Brahman tells her all
Glancing at Damayanti as he speaks.
"Damayanti, Nala's wife!
Oh it is you, my sister's daughter.
Why did we not see that little lotus bud
Between your brows?
We heeded not the sign
That beauty spot the Creator marked you with!
And yet my blood knew you from the moment
I set eyes upon you.
Come to me!"
She embraces Damayanti.
"Is it any wonder that
I felt such affection
For you Damayanti?"
I saw you when you were
Newly born,"
Says the Queen Mother joyfully.
"So long ago that was!

You do not recall my face
But we are of one blood."
"How well you have treated me
A stranger to your land, my mother's sister!
And you, Sunanda,
How well you have looked after me!
I have been more to you than a handmaid.
You have denied me nothing.
You have guarded my honour.
Yet there is another home dearer than this to me.
Allow me then, to leave for the
Home of my childhood
Where my children wait for me.
Too long have I been away.
Suhadeva tells me that they are much grown
How lonely they must be."
"You shall leave right now, if you so desire,
My sister's daughter.
I shall send with you a troop of my finest men.
You will enter your father's land royally escorted
Seated in my own favourite palanquin.
I fare you well, my kin.
May you find your Nala soon!"
She lays bejewelled fingers
On Damayanti's bowed head in blessing.

Kali's Lament - Part 12 - Reunion

Bearing Damayanti's message
Suhadeva hastens to the palace of
King Rituparna.
Outside in the courtyard, Nala
Accosts the Brahman.
Tears roll down his cheeks as
The twice-born repeats Damayanti's words,
"Where have you gone
You who abandoned me in the forest wild?
I wait for you
You who were called noble and true
Not so long ago!
Have you no compassion
No conscience?"
Nala, shame-faced and weeping
Misshapen Nala with the
Shrunken arm answers,
"Only a noblewoman may be composed in her
Great grief
And so win heaven by her many virtues.
She is invincible.
Nor will she give way to anger against her lord
Who deserted her
For he is in deep distress,

King without kingdom!"
Nala burns to leave all and seek her.
What torture to restrain himself from
Telling all to Vrishni!
He tires of it.
The Dice!
He must learn the skill of the Dice.
Damayanti, having received Nala's answer
Sends word about another *swayamvara*.
Only Nala would speak those words.
Only he could drive King Rituparna to Vidarbha
For her *swayamvara*
In a day's time.
Could the grotesque dwarf be her beloved
Made ugly under a curse?
The people wonder at Damayanti's
Sudden decision.
The loyal, suffering wife
Now suddenly decides to abandon the search
For her husband.
Nala is pained at the news.
Is this a ploy of Damayanti's
To bring him to her
Or has she truly ceased to love him and found
another, as he feared?
Women have fickle hearts.
Above all, he dreads the thought of
Driving King Rituparna
To the choosing ceremony of his beloved.

To watch her garland another in his presence.
Nala yokes the four horses to the King's chariot.
They are lean animals, nostrils wide and scarlet.
Flawless are they, bearing the
True marks of thoroughbreds.
The King, ready to mount the car
Frowns at Nala's choice.
"What do you mean by this, Vahuka?
This is no time for jesting.
How can these horses carry us a thousand miles
In a single day?"
"Each of these horses bears twelve curls, O King
One on the forehead, one on each temple
Four on the sides, four on the chest
One on the crest of its back.
I am sure these steeds will carry us
Like the wind to your heart's desire.
But if you would choose others
Point them out to me, and I shall
Yoke them instead."
"I am not as well versed in the
Science of horses as you are, Vahuka.
I trust your judgment.
Your success will be the ultimate proof of your
Skill with horses."
Vrishni mounts the chariot after the King.
Amazed at the dwarf's knowledge.
The horses fret, straining at the reins.
Nala soothes them with magical, liquid words.

He urges them forward, uttering sharp cries.
The hooves lift into the air.
Vrishni and the king gasp as the chariot
Skims over the Gate of the Sun.
Vrishni recalls the keen-eyed Matali,
Charioteer of the Gods.
Has he come to them in disguise?
Or has Vahuka learned this superhuman skill
From Nala?
Vrishni's mind reels in confusion.
Is it Nala himself
His beauty despoiled by some god's curse?
The chariot rushes across the skies,
A streak of lightning.
Over peaks and valleys, rivers,
Seas of green forest, cities, villages.
The wind sings and shrieks about them
Blowing their hair and garments backwards
Bending the horses' manes.
"I have never driven so swiftly," thinks Nala.
"The wind steals my breath.
All for Damayanti.
I come, beloved, wait for me!"
More than a quarter of the way later
The King's mantle is swept off his shoulders.
Fluttering like some angry red cloud
It settles gently to earth.
"Stop Vahuka!" he shouts above
The raging wind.

"Stop, so Vrishni may retrieve my mantle."
"We have already come five miles
From your mantle," answers Nala
Eyes brimming with Damayanti
"We will lose time if we return."
They are above the deep woods
When Rituparna, sighting a tall Vibhitak tree
Heavy with fruit, says eagerly:
"Slow down now, Vahuka!
Look at that tree.
On two of its branches, there are
Fifty million leaves
And two thousand and ninety berries.
I know not all there is to know
But this one thing – numbers and dice,
I am greatly skilled at
Just as you are at taming steeds
Making them fly like the wind."
Nala feels anticipation throb in his temples.
"Now is the time for learning," he thinks.
"I will not let it pass."
To Rituparna, he says, "I shall descend
And count for myself."
"Ah, but we cannot pause now.
There is not time enough for play."
"Then choose, O King, between Vrishni and I
As your charioteer.
The road lies straight and clear."
"That cannot be, Vahuka.

You are a matchless charioteer.
Only you could drive us to Vidarbha
By this eve.
If you will give me your word that we will
Reach in time for the *swayamvara*
You may do as you please."

The chariot falls like a leaf
Beside the Vibhitak tree.
Nala cuts the branches, hands shaking
With the excitement.
He counts with the speed of thought.
"Indeed, you are right, King.
Your gift is a marvel.
Teach it to me, Lord, I burn to know.
In return, I shall teach you my
Skills with horses."
His eyes gleam like a hungry child's.
"So be it."
They sit beneath the trees
Throwing the Dice.
Nala wins the second round and then
Suddenly falls to earth
Vomiting green rivulets of venom
I, Kali, am borne away
On the vile flood!
The agony of it makes him shake and cough
Until he is almost swooning with the ordeal.
"You are ill, Vahuka!

What is the matter?
Have you eaten something flawed?"
Says the King.
Varshneya, now more puzzled than ever
Runs to rub Nala's shaking shoulders.
I stand before them, yet only Nala sees me.
The curse begins to take shape in his mind.
His eyes are veined with red.
Yes, I am afraid of his curse.
I, the invincible Kali, am afraid.
The power of mortal curses is strange.
Even the immortals dare not ignore them.
What if he banishes me from this world?
How then will I behold Damayanti again?
I plead with him in shame.
I promise never to trouble him.
I tell him how I have suffered from
Damayanti's curses
The serpent's venom.
If I were Nala, I would not be swayed.
But he is merely mortal, soft!
As the last waves of agony sweep through him
He checks his thoughts
What have I come to?
Great immortal Kali, to grovel
At my enemy's feet!
Yet I must follow my enemy!
Keep my promises to him.
Promises are sacred even to the immortal.

Sacred even to evil.
Sacred too, to one trapped in maya.
For what is this feeling I nurture for
A mortal woman but maya?
Like a mortal have I become
Trapped in the net of maya.
I, who laughed at the mere idea of love,
Enamoured by a woman whom
I admire and despise!
Propping Nala's lolling head on his lap
Vrishni makes him drink a herb potion
The King watches anxiously
This incredible scene.
Vahuka, his brave, strong Vahuka
Thus violently ill!
Will he ever reach Vidarbha
In time for the *swayamvara*?
Nala rises at last
Mumbles an apology for this
Unforeseen delay
Climbs into the chariot, glowing gold beneath
Layers of dust.
His heart is bursting.
He dreams of her
He dreams of wearing the crown again.
He feels invincible.
Tears sting his eyes when
He thinks of his people.
He shouts words of magic at the horses.

The king sighs with relief.
The thunder begins.
The horses neigh
Tossing their broad-jawed heads
Nostrils flaring red
Flying hooves swifter after their rest.
The sun is a drop of blood
Hanging in the heavens
When they storm through Vidarbha's gates.
The palace looms up ahead.
Hearing the unmistakeable
Thunder of Nala's chariot
Damayanti runs to the roof of the palace
Certain that it is he.
Peacocks crane their iridescent necks and dance.
Her heart is like the cloud that thunders
At the approach of rain.
Who else can it be but her beloved?
She knows by the sound of the wheels
The horses' hooves.
The sound she thrilled to for many years.
"If it is not he," she whispers to the peacock,
"I shall perish by fire."
Damayanti presses her hands
To her heaving breast
As though to still the thunder.
She peers down breathless at the chariot
That has reared to a stop
In the middle of the courtyard.

She watches Vrishni descen
Followed by the King.
With mounting dread she watches for Nala.
That misshapen thing driving the car
Towards the stables!
He looks up to see her.
A smile lights his weary features.
She shivers.
He is Nala and he is not.
"Surely it is he that the Brahman
Described to me
He that uttered those meaningful words
Only as Nala would utter them!"
She shivers again,violently.
King Bhima is surprised at Rituparna's
Sudden appearance.
Welcoming him,he asks for
The reason of this visit.
Rituparna, amazed at seeing
No signs of a *swayamvara*,
No festivities, no kings
No princes come to woo Damayanti
And fearing some kind of stratagem
Answers wisely,
"I have come to pay my respects
To you, Bhima!"
And Damayanti?
Damayanti is torn by memories
Of her beautiful Nala.

How can she bring herself to love
This deformed thing?
How can she thrill to the touch of
Those warped hands?
Yet he is her beloved,is he not?
Perhaps the spell of the Evil One
Is still upon him
The reason for his ugliness.
She shall free him from the spell.
"Go, Kesni," she tells her hand maiden
"Go now and speak to that misshapen charioteer
I think he is my Nala.
And pay heed to his answer."
Kesni runs through the gardens
Towards the stables
Her breath tearing
Anklets jingling.
He hears her approach and turns
From the foaming horses
Hoping that it is Damayanti
Who has come to him.
"The Princess Damayanti asks to know
Who you may be and what brings you here,"
Says Kesni, gasping for breath.
"King Rituparna was told
That Damayanti is holding
A *swayamvara* at dawn tomorrow.
I drove him hither,swifter than the wind."
"Who is the third man with you?" asks Kesni

"His name is Vrishni.
He was King Nala's dearest friend once.
Now, after Nala's exile,
He serves King Rituparna.
I am Vahuka,
Skilled tamer of steeds
Preparer of the King's meals."
"Does Vrishni know about Nala's whereabouts?
Has he told you anything about Nala?"
"It was Vrishni who brought
Nala's children to safety
Here from Nishadha
But he knows nothing about him.
Indeed, no one knows about Nala.
He has been changed
Into a shape unrecognisable
And wanders about the world in this disguise
He will not reveal himself."
Kesni pauses,takes a deep breath.
"Do you remember Damayanti's message?
And the words you uttered in answer?"
"I remember them well."
"Repeat what you said to the Brahman,
I pray you
It will heal her grief!"
Overcome by emotion
He utters the words.
"Ah, but why so sorrowful
If you knew him not?"

She asks with the hint of a smile.
"I feel for him."
Nala thinks of the magic robe
The serpent god had given him.
Should he become his true self again?
Dare he appear before his beloved
In this grotesque disguise?
Surely she will recoil from his ugliness!
And what of the swayamvara?
Why does he see no signs of it?
Now he feels more certain that it is
Damayanti's desperate way
To reunite them.
Surely she must know that he would
Come to claim her
From the ends of the earth!
Yet how can he be sure?
He must tread cautiously.
"Watch the dwarf closely, Kesni,"
Says Damayanti,"when
He prepares the royal meal.
See that none give him fire or water."
For Nala,rich with the gifts of the gods
Needs not these things.
Kesni watches amazed as Nala enters
The low portals of the servants' dwellings
And the portals rise to let him in.
She watches, unseen,
As he gazes upon the empty vessels

And they are filled with water.
He holds up a handful of
Withered grass to the sun
Gazes intently upon it and it bursts into flames
Leaving his fingers unscorched.
He picks up dying flowers
And they bloom once again
Their fragrance richer than before.
This she conveys to Damayanti
Who weak at the knees
Sinks to the bed
Her heart beating wild.
She is certain it is he.
No other has these special god given powers.
Yet she cannot tell her children that
This dwarf is their beautiful sire.
How see her beloved in those beady eyes
Hidden by flesh
The flattened nose
The hanging lips?
Will her love take flight at the sight
Of such ugliness?
Yet miraculously the dwarf could turn into the
Nala she loves
The Nala whose touch makes
A thousand flowers bloom
Beneath her skin
Whose lips are sweet.
"Take the children to the kitchens, Kesni,"

She says."Perhaps Nala will
Reveal himself to them
If not to me."
Kesni leads the children by the hand
Into the vast smoky kitchens.
Nala sees them, drops the stirrer, rushes to them
Goes down on his knees
Embraces them tenderly.
Sobbing,he holds them
To his breast a long while.
"Why weep? They are not your children,"
Says Kesni.
"Ah,these beautiful children
Remind me of my own,fair maiden.
I could not keep my tears at sight of them.
Take them away now
A princess' progeny should
Not enter the kitchens."
The children!
Little pieces of his heart!
How long it seems since he has heard
Their heart wrenching laughter
Seen the gleam in their large, innocent eyes!
Does Damayanti seek his response to them
Knowing that he must respond?
Or have they come to see
The ugly dwarf the palace whispers about?
Ah, lovers believe what they want to believe!
Hope cuts through him like a knife.

Does Damayanti suspect that he is her beloved?
But how could she forgive him
For abandoning her?
She would never believe he ever loved her.
He had succumbed to the Evil One
He had been weak
His mind and heart not strong enough
To battle Kali.
He wipes his tears on a grimy sleeve
Rises to his feet.
"Come to the palace, the Princess asks for you."
"For me?"he feels a jolt of joy in his belly
"How can I, a lowly charioteer
Enter the royal chambers?"
"It is her command, come!"
The sight of Damayanti
Standing outside the palace doors
In scarlet robes
Her hair tangled, the mourning mark of ashes
On her fair forehead, makes his head reel.
How beautiful she is
How sad and distant
Like some ice maiden
Surrounded by empty vastnesses of snow.
Why has she summoned him?
To question him about King Rituparna
To ask him to entertain the court
With his comic ugliness
To commend him for riding like the wind

Just as her beloved would?
He longs to touch her
Throw his arms around her.
But surely,she will draw away from him.
He waits for her words
Like parched earth waits for rain.
"O Vahuka," she says in trembling tones
"Have you heard of the man
Just and noble who abandoned his sleeping wife
In a forest wild?
How could he abandon the woman
Who chose him above the gods?
What fault was it of mine
That he left me
Mother of his children?
Is this how he keeps his marriage vows?"
"That is not true, Princess!
The evil Kali possessed me then
When I played the Dice.
He possessed me when I deserted you.
He made me bend to his evil will.
Your curses made him suffer greatly
But he stayed in possession of my soul
Till the venom of Karkotaka
And my new knowledge of the Dice
Drove him from me.
O beautiful Damayanti, beloved,
Our sorrows are at an end.
I have come here at great speed

To find you again
I had greatly feared that you
Would not forgive me
That you would choose another.
Three years of estrangement from you
My beloved
And then came news about the *swayamvara*!
I did not know what to believe!"
She trembles at his words.
"Blame me not,Nala!
I am not guilty of such a shameful thought.
I wanted to lure you here
After the Brahman brought me your message
I knew you would come if I were
To hold another *swayamvara*.
May the wind draw away my breath
If I do not speak true, my husband
For I have always been faithful to you.
Let the sun steal away its warmth from my limbs
Let the pale moon deny me peace
If I have sinned!
O let them speak for me
Or abandon me,beloved!"
The wind whistles around them.
Nala listens, all his senses
Centred on his hearing.
He hears the soughing of the wind:
"O Nala, Damayanti has done no evil.
Faithful has she remained to you for

The three years of your estrangement.
You have found her.
Now do not be foolish enough
To lose her again!"
Flowers fall
The music of the spheres begins.
Nala dons his magic robe
Calls upon Karkotaka.
Desire stirs in Damayanti's veins
Those sweet purple veins
On the inside of her
Fair rounded arms.
She feels his embrace engulf her.
Everything seems glad at this reunion.
The singing birds
The swaying trees
The very stones.
But I burn as though the snake vermin's venom
Courses through me still.
Not for me the silk of her skin.
For I have no hands.

Antara Unleashed -
And Yet. And Yet.

I liked the way Karan did my face. He said it
was therapy for him. A face was a canvas, he
said. He was discovering my many faces: coy,
sexy, delicate, demure, tough, sophisticated,
little girl. I liked the wild disarray of lipsticks,
brushes and eye shadows and all those magic
ointments that transformed me over and over
again. I found a sensual pleasure in the tickle of
the brush upon my lips, the caress of rouge, the
coolness of eyeliner, Karan blowing upon my
eyelids magic gold, magenta and turquoise,
breathing success into my soul, my very pores.
Applause crashed like thunder, a validation I
craved. Daring costumes became second skin,
defying expectations. Defying rules. Feathers
and silk. Top hats. Black lace garters, elegant
gloves up to my arms. Diva gowns inspired by
Hollywood. Punk hairdo streaked red. The girls,
once rivals, could not deny the power I wielded.
And Mama, who once called me ugly, where
was she? See this woman, this creature of
vibrant hues and audacious lines—this is what
you couldn't see.

And yet. And yet.

I looked at myself in the mirror that stood next
to the human skull my medical student boyfriend
had given me. I lit candles inside it to heighten

the air of magic and mystery I thrived on. But one night, the stench of burning bone seeped into my slumber and created a nightmare. I saw a man hitting a woman on the head with an object that looked like a cricket bat. I jerked awake and put the candle out. I never blew out candles. It was an insult to the salamander of the element of fire. One of my books on magic had told me that. Before I put out the flame, I glimpsed in the orange glow, a terrified face. This time as I dressed for my date, and slid the red lipstick across my kiss-bruised lips, I thought how like a clown I seemed with my painted eyes and lips, my sorrow over father's death still sharp and green under my skin, and I wept. The clown face crumbled. But the tears were few. I had always had control over my tears. Like Rilke's angels with weary mouths. Faerie doomed to a frantic, sometimes shallow happiness. Like lonely women who shed only seven tears into the sea to summon a selkie lover.

Antara Unleashed - Resurrection

How end a chapter that has never been written?

They say Mama took the bus to Varanasi and
killed herself there.

Why did she choose Varanasi with its burning
ghats and its million gods in a million shrines?
She was Christian.

I see her at the rear of the trundling bus, so
omnipresent that I see no one else. Pale, weary,
no make-up, tear-stained, in a pale, weary sari,
no pink roses on the white gossamer organza,
just a forgotten yellowing. I wept long when I
heard about her lonely suicide.

I feel the white organza between my fingers. She
had painted pink roses on it. All I have left of
her is this sari, a tiny mascara brush, spools of
her practising French and a small journal filled
with her writing.

She would beat me with steel hangers and
brushes for watching her transform her lovely
face in front of her dressing table. I am reading
her words for the first time, and before the
yellowing pages fall to pieces, I write them here
for you and for myself. Her handwriting is

beautiful. Her words are too, as though she were
not quite herself when she wrote them.

'I called his name in the silence
From the depths of a lonely grief
He did not speak, but a bird sang out
And I knew a strange relief.

I sought his face in the forest
Where we walked
In the days gone by
He hid from me
But I saw a birch
Green and silver against the sky.

He comes like this
In the beauty of a song, a flower or a tree
And who am I to attempt to solve
So great a mystery?'

Was she writing about God? Was she writing
about a love lost?

'They loved one another
Yet neither
Would tell the other
So with love

They were almost heartbroken
Yet looked upon each other as foes.

They parted at last
And sometimes
Though only in dreams
They met
They had long been dead
Those lovers
But themselves
Scarce knew it yet.'

Mama rewrote the poems in her journal. Were
they affirmations?
Her last words scribbled at the back are:
'Pax vobiscum
Peace be with you.'
Did she anticipate my reading her words?

It is a strange coincidence, or perhaps none, that
my sister killed herself too and wrote similar
lines in her journal. Perhaps the depressed stay
afloat on such words.

There were times when we sisters were one.
When we hunted for the wild blackberries the
sunning lizards so loved to gobble; chased
butterflies; gathered the succulent mangoes

felled by the hot dust-laden winds of summer,
and tried to capture the fairies of the Dandelion.

On Diwali, the Festival of Lights, we fought
over the iridescent pink and blue clay pots and
pans and stoves and tiny platters and spoons and
the white porous, crumbly candy and puffed
rice. The gigantic house was transformed into a
fairy tale castle, glittering with hundreds of
flames, lit to welcome back home from exile,
Lord Rama. The skies were glorious with stars
that fell to earth, trailing glory; a smell of
sulphur lit the air. But we never loved each other
as sisters should.

I was grateful to mother at Christmas. Enchanted
nights, filled with the voices of angels singing
Silent Night, Holy Night, as I lay half asleep. I
yearned to know the truth about Santa Claus, no
matter how it hurt. In the darkness, I heard the
reindeer bells and looked up at the ventilator to
catch a glimpse of Santa's white beard. I closed
my eyes quickly. Mama had warned me not to
let Santa catch me peeking. It would make him
go away forever. How hard my heart beat on that
Christmas Eve!

Mama took us to the roof the morning after Christmas Eve and showed us the tracks of Santa's sleigh circling the chimney.

When I did discover the bitter truth about Santa, it was the end of Christmas. That night of the great and painful discovery, I spied father pushing some large packages under my bed. Mama was furious with me for finding out. I realised then the love and effort she had put into making Christmas so special for us. It was she who had etched the sleigh marks around the chimney; it was she who had rung the bells. But now, there would be no more nights sweet with the voices of angels.

Yet Mama lives because of the scars she inflicted on me from a deep despair and hopefully, love.

She was the one who made me the woman I am today – the priestess of the moon goddess, the femme fatale, the breaker of hearts, the sexy bodhisattva who lures men to the Path, not to herself, the writer of stories that make strangers weep, the painter painting beautiful punks with spiked hair with their Great Danes in their gardens, Goth fashionistas with magnificent

head-dresses fleeing from the Sand Worm of
Dune, its teeth like those in the mouths of baleen
whales, beautiful long-legged witches in black
gowns brewing magic, and The Buddha, The
Buddha who brought a courtesan to her knees
and a collector of severed thumbs to his
enlightenment.

She was the one who told me of the enchantment
of the Mulberry Tree, the feathery seeds of the
dandelion that are really fairies.

It was the mulberry tree I loved best. I sat on its
kind branches, my lips, my clothes stained with
the purple juice of the fruit. Everything I
touched turned purple – my white dress, the
cherished pages of the red-bound picture bible,
the drawing book filled with my childish
sketches.

At my touch, the enchanted trunk of the
mulberry tree parted down the middle. At its
core stood the Red Fairy Mama told me about.
"We've been expecting you," she said in a
musical voice, and taking my hand in her warm,
lovely one, led me within.

"I knew you were real," I said, the smell of the
wood sweet in my nostrils.

The Red Fairy had translucent red wings with
veins of gold. She smiled all the time. I noticed
her high cheekbones, her oval face so like mine,
her dark, slanting eyes. Upon her red hip-length
hair sat a ruby tiara; her dress was red, her
delicate ankles encircled with anklets of rubies.
She led me from the twilight of the tree's core to
the moonlight of another realm.

Tiny greenish lights flitted among strange,
crooked trees with bark of silver and gold.
"Fireflies," said the Red Fairy. " They light our
homes." She held out her long, delicate fingers,
and the lights hovered over them.

Then the music began, and hundreds of small,
slender, shining figures began to dance in a
circle beneath the moon.
"It is just as Mama said it would be, as I
imagined it to be," I thought, my feet tapping to
the music of fairy flutes and lyres. A swing hung
from the clouds. "I would so like to fly to
heaven on your swing," I said to the Red Fairy.

"Here all your dreams come true, dear child."
Her tenderness brought tears to my eyes, for it
had been a long time since I had seen

tenderness. "I have the feeling you are looking for someone, something."

"I do not know. You must possess something before you can lose it. What have I possessed?"

"I will show you," said the Red Fairy, and taking my hand led me into a vast field of pink roses; the roses Mama had painted on her sari. I walked among them slowly, not flinching when thorns scratched at my legs. I entered a cloud of fireflies. A woman lay where they hovered like stars. Her arms lay crossed upon a breast that was still as stone. Pink rose petals covered her eyelids.

"No!" I cried, and kneeling beside her, kissed her quickly on the lips. The rose petals fell upon her cheeks as she opened her eyes. Arms reached for me, rocked me upon a sobbing breast. "My child, my poor child!" she whispered, and I felt, for the first time, her hot tears upon my face. After a few moments, she set me down among the roses and, with a smile I had never before seen, said, "Let us play together."

Hand in hand, we ran towards the red swing that hung from the moonlit skies; pink roses sprang wherever Mama stepped, and I knew she was transformed. Breathless and laughing, she sat upon the swing, and lifting me onto her warm lap, began to swing, her feet pushing against the earth. Higher and higher we rose until the moon seemed only a leap away, and I saw behind a silver-limned cloud the angel who had wiped away my tears with his great soft wings long ago in that cold, dark room.

He was brighter than the moon, and he was laughing too.